3/09

LIVER CANCER

Current and Emerging Trends in Detection and Treatment

TAMRA B. ORR

ROSEN
PUBLISHING®

New York

Published in 2009 by The Rosen Publishing Group, Inc.
29 East 21st Street, New York, NY 10010

First Edition

Library of Congress Cataloging-in-Publication Data

Orr, Tamra B.
Liver cancer: current and emerging trends in detection and treatment / Tamra B. Orr.—1st ed.
    p. cm.—(Cancer and modern science)
Includes bibliographical references and index.
ISBN-13: 978-1-4358-5009-5 (library binding)
1. Liver—Cancer—Popular works. I. Title.
RC280.L5O76 2008
616.99'436—dc22

                                                    2008019939

Manufactured in the United States of America

On the cover: A light micrograph of a section of liver reveals two cancerous tumors (dark crimson) surrounded by healthy tissue (lighter red). This is a secondary, or metastasized, carcinoma, meaning the cancer has spread to the liver from another site in the body.

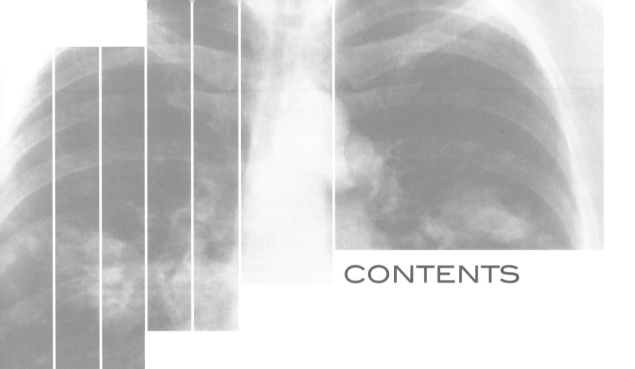

CONTENTS

INTRODUCTION

The human body is remarkably adept at surviving. If you lose vision in one eye or hearing in one ear, then you have another matched organ just waiting to take over. Lose a kidney, and there's another one ready to take on the duties of both. Lose your tonsils or appendix, and you can easily survive without them.

All of that comes to a halt with the liver. On the one hand, it is the most resilient organ in your body. It is often nicknamed the "powerhouse of the body." The philosopher Socrates once referred to the liver as "the seat of the soul."

A liver can get injured or be partly removed, and it will actually grow back. It can even change size according to its host. For example, a baboon liver that is transplanted into a human grows to the size of a human liver. A liver from a large dog that is transplanted into that of a very small dog will shrink to the proper size. Injure this organ enough, however, through a lifetime of alcohol abuse or a bad viral infection, and it may not be able to function properly anymore.

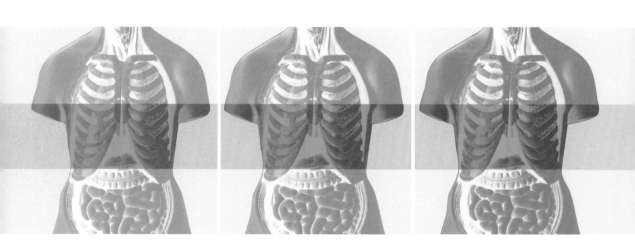

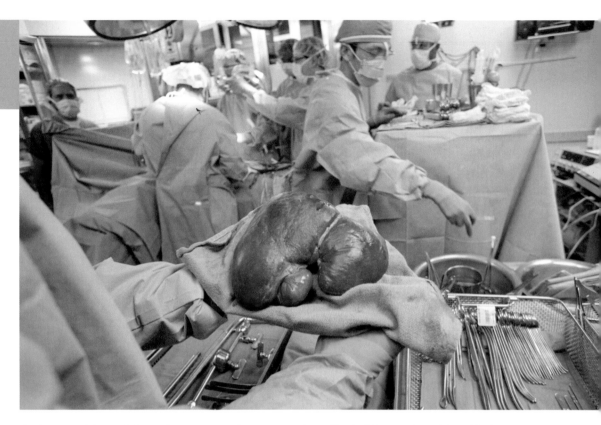

A diseased liver (above) is surgically removed at Tisch Hospital in New York University's Medical Center.

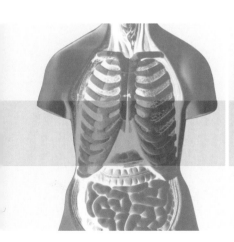
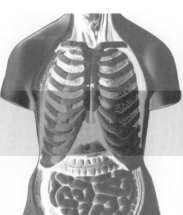
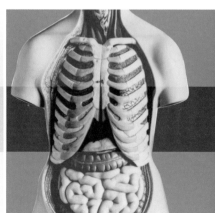

Life without your liver simply isn't possible. It is in charge of so many different duties that, should it quit working, you would die within twenty-four hours. If it becomes sick or is hit with a disease such as cancer, then it can create havoc throughout the body, disrupting or interfering with many functions.

Liver cancer is a diagnosis that thousands of people a year receive from their physicians. It is the third most common cause of cancer deaths. Experts predict that in 2008, more than 18,400 people will lose their lives to this disease. How does this cancer begin? And what chances do people have to survive it? To answer these questions, let's look through the laboratory microscope and observe surgeons at work.

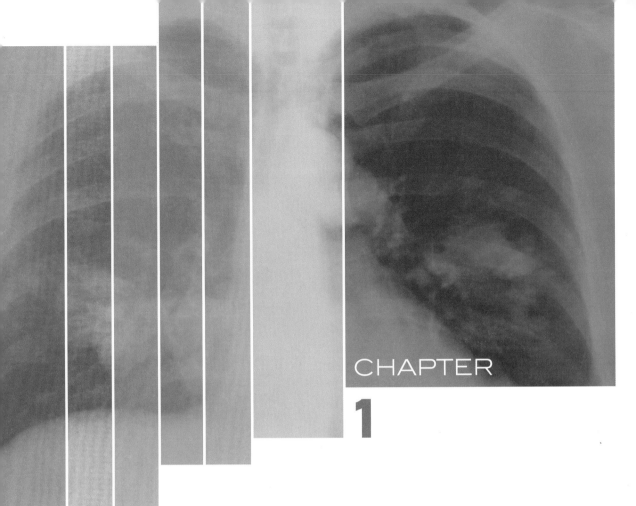

ALL ABOUT THE LIVER

The human body is made up of many different organs. A number of them specialize in one particular aspect of keeping a person alive and well. The heart, for example, is essential to having blood circulate throughout the body and getting oxygen to every cell. The lungs ensure that people can breathe in "good" air and get rid of "bad" air. Bones keep our bodies from becoming puddles on the ground—they provide a rigid structure upon which our muscles, skin, and organs can hang. Muscles, in turn, make sure those bones can bend and move with ease, while also protecting them from breakage.

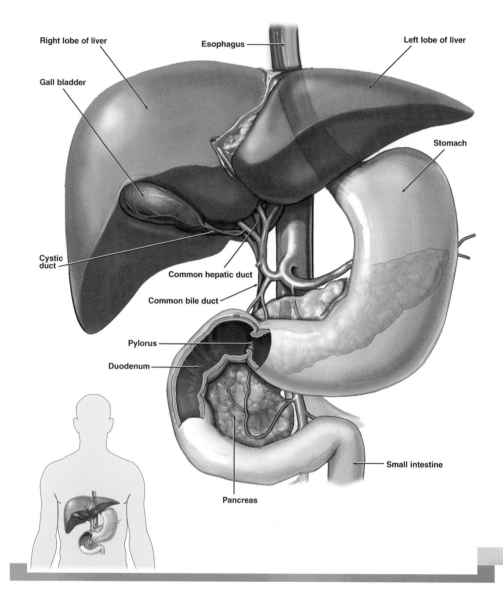

The two lobes of the liver are shown here, as is the liver's relationship to other nearby digestive organs, including the stomach, esophagus, gall bladder, bile duct, pancreas, and small intestine.

What does the liver do? After all, it must have an important job because it is the biggest organ in the body. It weighs between 3 and 4 pounds (about 2 kilograms) and is the size of a football. Shaped a little like a triangle, it is located right behind the ribs on the right side of your abdomen. It is just above the stomach but below the diaphragm. If you press in at the bottom of your ribs and curl your fingers up, then you can often feel the bottom part of your liver.

A GREEK TITAN

The power of the liver has been known for centuries. This can be seen in one of the Greek gods' most common myths.

Prometheus was a Titan in the world of Greek gods. He made the mistake of defying the all-powerful Zeus, however, and he paid a steep price for it. It was Prometheus's job to help humans evolve. To do this, he felt they needed the gift of fire. Zeus disagreed. Fire belonged only to the gods. Prometheus ignored this and showed humans how to harness the power of fire, radically changing and improving their lives.

Zeus was furious, so he punished Prometheus by chaining him to the top of a mountain and sending an eagle down each morning to peck out and eat the Titan's liver. Because the liver has the ability to regenerate, or grow back, it would be intact by the next morning. Therefore, the eagle would come back and consume Prometheus's liver all over again. This endless torture did not stop until the Greek hero Hercules rescued Prometheus from this terrible fate.

This rendering of the internal structure of the liver reveals the thousands of lobules (the small, gray, hexagonal structures) that connect to ducts (the blue squiggly channels) that ultimately link to the hepatic duct (the large blue channel), which carries waste out of the liver and into the gall bladder and duodenum.

The liver is a reddish-brown color and is divided into sections called lobes. The right lobe is slightly larger than the left one. It is constantly filling up with and distributing blood. The blood is brought to the liver by the hepatic portal vein and the hepatic artery. The portal vein carries nutrient-rich blood from the intestines to the liver, while the artery brings blood that is rich in oxygen. The blood leaves the liver through a hepatic vein.

Each of the two main lobes is made up of thousands of smaller lobes, or lobules. They are shaped like hexagons, meaning that they have six sides like a stop sign. Each one of these little lobules, in turn, is made up of liver cells, known as hepatocytes. Hepatocytes line up in rows. In between each one are tiny blood vessels that send oxygen and nutrients into the cells.

JUGGLING MANY JOBS

The liver actually performs more than three hundred separate functions within the body. Here are a few of the most important ones:

- **Bile production:** Bile is a greenish-brown fluid that is made in the liver. It doesn't sound nice, but it is essential for us to live. Bile plays a large role in the process of digesting fats. The liver makes it, the gallbladder stores it, and then the small intestine uses it to help with digestion.
- **Nutrient processing:** The liver processes the nutrients that it has absorbed from the small intestine, including vitamins A, D, E, and K. It then determines how much sugar, protein, and fat should enter the bloodstream.
- **Manufacture of blood-clotting substances:** The liver makes many proteins called clotting factors. These help the body to form and regulate blood clotting when blood vessels are injured.
- **Detoxification:** The liver is what keeps a person from suffering from overexposure to toxins. For example, it is the liver that filters drugs (recreational, over-the-counter, and prescription) and alcohol from the bloodstream. It can take on elements that are poisonous and make them safe, allowing people to get rid of them through their urine. It can even filter out the nasty elements found in some environments, such as secondhand cigarette smoke, air pollution, and lawn care chemicals.

——— **Storage of iron, vitamin B12, and copper for whenever the body needs it:** The liver is an amazing storage unit. It knows what to hold on to in case humans suddenly need an emergency supply of nutrients.

——— **Manufacturing of cholesterol:** Despite all the cholesterol-busting medications that you see advertised on TV, the body does need a certain amount of cholesterol in order to stay healthy. Cholesterol helps maintain healthy blood cell walls, it produces hormones, and it makes vitamin D. The liver is where it is manufactured.

——— **Blood sugar regulation:** Keeping your blood sugar levels as steady as possible is another duty of the liver. If it didn't do this, then a person could quickly become diabetic. The liver takes glucose, or blood sugar, and changes it into glycogen to store it. When the body needs an extra burst of energy, the liver changes it back to glucose and sends it out.

——— **Bacteria removal and immune system booster:** The liver produces elements that help the body fight off infection. It's even able to strip bacteria out of the bloodstream.

——— **Ammonia conversion:** When proteins are digested in the body, they create ammonia, which is toxic. The liver changes the ammonia into a less toxic form called urea. It then sends the urea off to the kidneys to be excreted the next time you urinate.

If any one of these liver functions were interrupted, then it's easy to imagine the trouble and chaos that would follow. Blood wouldn't clot, or its reserves would be depleted. Toxins would overwhelm the body. Digestion would slow and even stop. Energy would be practically nonexistent, and immunity would be threatened.

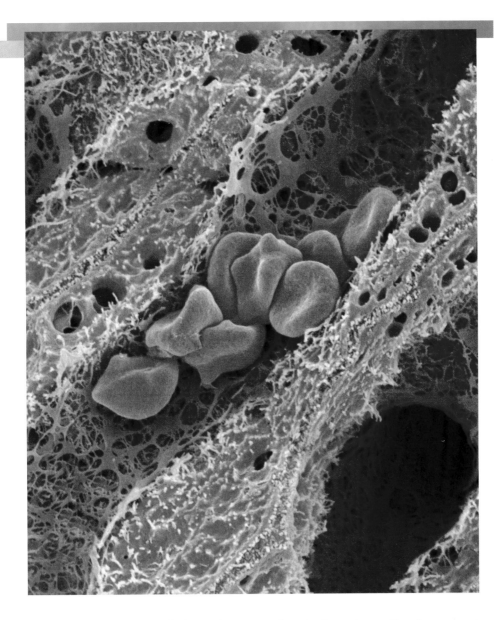

In this image, red blood cells lie within a capillary in liver tissue. The liver contains 10 percent of the body's blood supply.

PROTECTING THE LIVER

Clearly, if the liver is this important to your body, then it needs to be protected as much as possible from damage. What threatens the liver more than anything? Unnecessary medications and alcohol top the list. Because the liver is responsible for dealing with toxic substances, the more it has to deal with, the more risk there is for trouble. While certain medications are essential for people to manage different health conditions, there are also some drugs that should be used sparingly, if at all. For example, taking too much acetaminophen (Tylenol) on a regular basis is enough to damage the liver. If a person can avoid reaching for these types of pills every time something hurts, the liver would appreciate it.

Alcohol is definitely one of the worst offenders for livers. It takes a lot of effort on the part of the liver to deal with alcohol—whether it is beer, wine, or liquor. If alcohol is consumed every day, even in small amounts, then it can set up a great many problems, including a higher risk for conditions such as liver cancer.

What you eat on a daily basis is another factor that can help or hurt your liver. Eating a lot of fatty or deep-fried foods, for example, not only makes the waistline grow but also increases the risk of digestive problems in the gallbladder and liver. Helpful lifestyle choices that support a healthy liver include keeping your weight down and getting regular exercise.

TOP LIVER FACTS

1. The liver produces between 400 and 800 mL of bile every single day.

2. The liver can hold up to 13 percent of the body's entire blood supply due to its many blood vessels.

3. There are more than six hundred medicines (prescription and over-the-counter) that are harmful to the liver.

4. The liver filters out environmental toxins such as air pollutants, pesticides, secondhand cigarette smoke, and chemicals, turning them into products that are discarded through the urine.

5. The liver pulses much like a heart beats. It has to do this in order to cope with the massive quantities of blood that pass through it every minute of every day.

6. The liver keeps a store of iron, vitamin B12, and copper for whenever your body needs it.

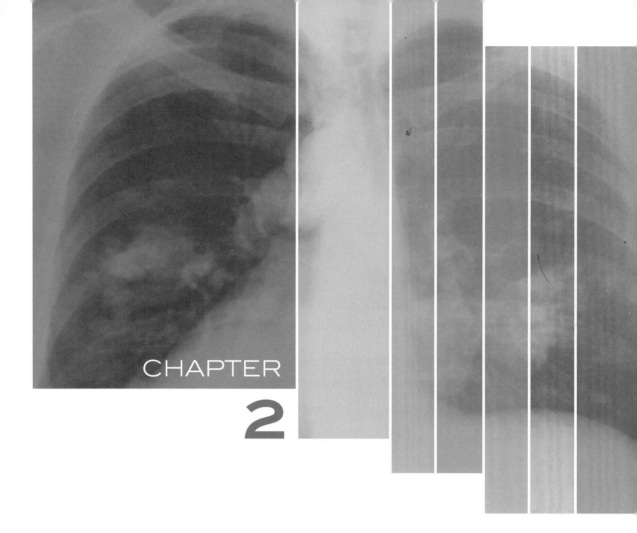

SIGNS AND SYMPTOMS OF TROUBLE

Liver cancer is often called a "silent killer." Why? Because many times, the symptoms of liver cancer do not show up until the problem is rather advanced. This makes it hard for physicians to catch it early, when there is still time to do something about it. The sobering fact about liver cancer is that the majority of people who are diagnosed with it will die from it within a year. It is a very serious condition. Ideally, cancer treatment is designed to eliminate the disease—or at least slow down its growth. With some more lethal cancers, however, treatment is more focused on easing the condition's symptoms instead of curing the disease itself.

This book will focus on primary liver cancer, which, simply put, is cancer that starts in the liver and either stays there or can spread to other parts of the body through the circulatory or lymphatic system. Liver cancer is not common but is generally quite deadly. Secondary liver cancer, on the other hand, is just the opposite. But, unfortunately, it is occurring more often and is likely due to substance overuse, like alcohol, and certain viral infections of the liver (hepatitis).

SYMPTOMS OF LIVER CANCER

Sadly, liver cancer is a condition that does not have a clear cause. Physicians believe the DNA of the liver cells becomes damaged somehow, triggering a change in cell growth. They are not sure why the hepatocytes suddenly begin growing out of control and forming a mass. They only know that it happens, and in the majority of cases, that mass is malignant, or cancerous.

So, how does a person know that something is going wrong within his or her liver? The most common symptoms are:

— General, chronic loss of appetite
— Unintended weight loss
— Abdominal pain, particularly in the upper-right side by the ribs, with possible radiating pain to the right back and shoulder
— Nausea and vomiting
— Constant weakness and fatigue
— An enlarged, swollen liver
— Abdominal swelling due to water retention
— Yellow discoloration of the eyes and skin (jaundice)
— Swollen "spidery" veins that are easily seen through the skin (called varices and telangiectasias)
— Dark yellow, gold, or brown urine
— Itchy skin

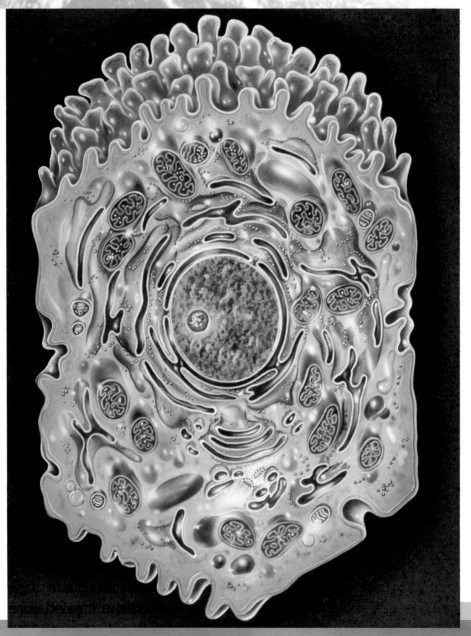

A liver cell, or hepatocyte, is pictured above with its various inner structures. The round brown mass in the center is the cell's nucleus. The tubules surrounding it synthesize blood proteins, while the green structures are bile capillaries that flush out waste.

Any of these symptoms could have a number of other causes. But when several of them appear together, it is a strong indication that testing for liver disease, including cancer, is the next step to take.

TYPES OF LIVER CANCER

Liver cancer is divided into several different types based on where the cancer cells originated. The most common type is hepatocellular carcinoma, which comes from the liver cells. Hepatocellular carcinoma can be a single tumor that continues to get bigger, or it can be several smaller tumors. The second type of primary liver cancer is cholangio-carcinoma. It begins in the small, tube-like bile ducts. A much rarer form of liver cancer is hepatoblastoma, which usually only occurs in young children and forms from very primitive liver cells. Another rare type is angiosarcoma, which is also known as heman-giosarcoma. It is a cancer of blood vessels and tends to grow very rapidly. People with this type of cancer often live fewer than six months.

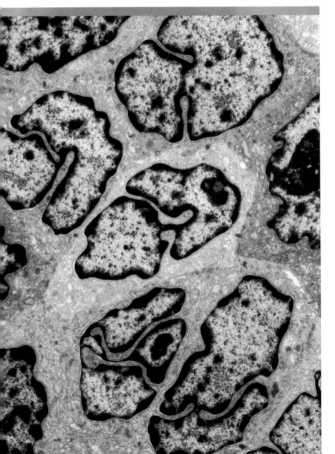

Liver cancer cells that are part of a hepatocellular carcinoma appear here. These cancer cells form in the lining of the liver and are associated with cirrhosis.

WHO IS AT RISK?

People of all ages and races can get liver cancer, but there are definite risk factors that raise the chances. For example, Asian Americans and immigrants from Asia have the highest risk of liver cancer. Hispanics and African Americans are second, while Caucasians are third. Men are twice as likely to develop liver cancer as women (likely because men are more likely to abuse alcohol), especially those who are over the age of sixty. Ninety percent of those diagnosed with liver cancer are between the ages of forty-five and eighty-five. A family history of liver problems, along with smoking and obesity, can raise the overall risk as well.

Other risk factors have more to do with the general health of the liver itself. For example, if a person has had chronic liver infections or hepatitis, then the risk is substantially higher. In fact, chronic hepatitis is the number one risk for developing liver cancer. Although there are vaccines for hepatitis A and B, there is none for type C, which is commonly contracted through the sharing of contaminated needles or by having sex with someone who is infected.

Another health problem that can injure the liver and increase the risk of developing liver cancer is cirrhosis. Cirrhosis occurs when liver cells are replaced over time with scar tissue. It's usually the result of years of abuse of alcohol, drugs, or other chemicals. Approximately 5 percent of those with cirrhosis will eventually develop liver cancer.

Conditions like primary biliary cirrhosis (inflammation of the bile ducts), often seen in association with ulcerative colitis (an autoimmune inflammation of the colon and digestive tract), increase the risk of liver cancer. An inherited condition such as hemochromatosis, in which the body absorbs too much iron from food, can be a factor, as can obesity, diabetes, and the use of anabolic steroids. Some doctors have also

Three types of human livers appear above. The left one is fatty. The middle one is cirrhotic. The right one is healthy.

suggested that there may be a link between liver cancer and the use of birth control pills or tobacco.

Other threats to the liver include exposure to aflatoxin, a substance that is created by certain types of mold that can form on peanuts, corn, nuts, and grain. This is a problem that doesn't occur as often in the United States because strict laws forbid allowing products into the country that may contain aflatoxins. It is a much bigger problem in countries in Asia and Africa. Exposure to other chemicals, including vinyl chloride (a chemical used to manufacture plastics), thorium dioxide (a chemical once given to people during X-ray examinations), and arsenic (sometimes found in well water), also raises the risk of developing liver cancer.

CANCER PROTECTION

Are there any steps that a person can take to reduce his or her risk of one day developing liver cancer? Yes, although they certainly hold no guarantee. Some positive steps to take include:

— Get the hepatitis A and B vaccines, as they offer almost 90 percent protection against these liver-damaging infections.

— Learn all you can about the health of the liver and the risks to its proper functioning.

— If you are sexually active, then make sure you always use a condom, which guards against sexually transmitted diseases, including hepatitis C.

— Never take intravenous drugs.

— Avoid body piercing and tattoos, as needles always carry a risk of passing on blood-borne diseases and infections such as hepatitis.

— Avoid alcohol.

— Avoid medications that injure the liver, like over-the-counter pain relievers.

While there is no way to be 100 percent safe from any kind of cancer, making some simple and easy lifestyle choices can certainly give you a better chance of not becoming another statistic.

MYTHS AND FACTS

MYTH Liver disease is always caused by alcohol abuse.

FACT One in ten Americans is affected by liver disease. There are more than ninety forms of liver disease, including liver cancer. Only some of these forms of liver disease are related to alcohol consumption. Causes of liver cancer can include genetics, hereditary disorders, obesity, hepatitis virus infection, cirrhosis (a liver disease that is not always alcohol-related), and exposure to aflatoxin B1 (a product of mold) and certain drugs, medicines, and chemicals.

MYTH **The symptoms of liver cancer will be obvious, so if I feel nothing unusual, then I have nothing to worry about.**

FACT Often, symptoms of liver cancer don't start showing up until the later stages of the disease's progression, when treatment options are few and the prognosis is poor. Symptoms can include fatigue, pain on the right side of the upper abdomen or around the right shoulder blade, nausea, loss of appetite, unexplained weight loss, and jaundice. If you have any of these symptoms, then see your doctor immediately.

MYTH **There is no cure or effective treatment for liver cancer.**

FACT If discovered early, liver cancer can be cured. Plus, new drugs and treatments are currently being tested that may soon offer either a cure or prolonged life for patients.

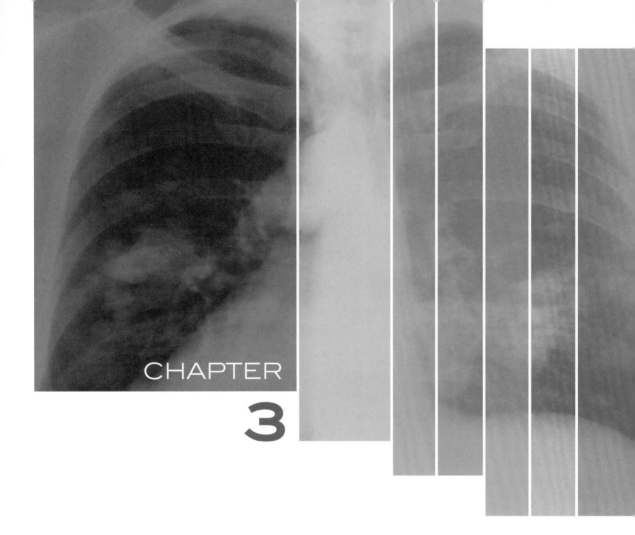

TESTS, EXAMS, AND DIAGNOSES

One of the first indications that something may be wrong with a person's liver often shows up through blood tests. It may reveal that a person has hepatitis (inflammation of the liver), for example, which is often a first step in liver illness. However, there are a number of different ways to find out if a person has primary liver cancer or not, and complete testing is necessary to make a diagnosis. Since it can be a scary diagnosis to make, physicians make sure they have all the medical evidence that they need before delivering the news to patients.

STARTING TO INVESTIGATE

The first step to finding out if there is a problem with the liver is a simple and noninvasive one: a physician sits down and gets a thorough medical history on a patient. This process often reveals vital clues as to what might be wrong. For instance, what does family history have to show? What are the symptoms? Are they mild, moderate, or severe? How long have these symptoms been bothersome?

Next is a basic physical examination. It will look at such simple things as blood pressure, pulse, height, and weight. The doctor will also palpate, or carefully feel, the abdomen. He or she will check the liver, spleen, and other organs to see if there are changes in the shape or size, or if there is a lump. The doctor will most likely check for ascites, an abnormal amount of fluid building up in the abdomen. He or she will examine a patient's skin and eyes to see if any yellow tinges can be seen, which would be an indication of jaundice and poor liver function.

After this initial basic examination, the doctor will start to do some more specific tests, which will be discussed next.

BLOOD TESTS

Commonly, a doctor will order a CBC, or complete blood count, because it can reveal so much information about a person's health. The CBC will measure:

- Hematocrit: the volume of red blood cells as a percentage of total blood volume.
- Hemoglobin: the number of grams of red blood cells in a sample of blood.
- Platelet count: the number of platelets, which affects the blood's ability to clot.

Here, a lab technician enters information derived from a patient's blood test into a computer for analysis. The results of the blood test and its analysis will help a doctor make an accurate diagnosis.

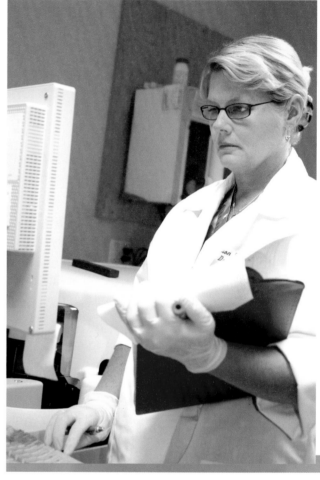

- White blood count: the number of white blood cells (if elevated, it can indicate an infection or inflammation somewhere in the body).

In addition to these, specific liver function blood tests will be ordered, including:

- Liver function tests (LFTs): measurements of liver enzymes (AST and ALT), alkaline phosphatase, albumin, GGT (gamma glutamyltransferase), and bilirubin.
- Coagulation studies: PT (protime) and PTT (partial thromboplastin time), which measure how well the blood clots and how well the liver is making normal blood clotting proteins.
- AFP (alpha-fetoprotein): a test to determine the level of alpha-fetoprotein in the blood, which can be suggestive of certain

types of live cancer. Although this is a somewhat helpful test, it is not always reliable because some tumors do not produce as much AFP as others do, leading to false readings. Other rare types of tumors, such as germ cell tumors, can also produce AFP.

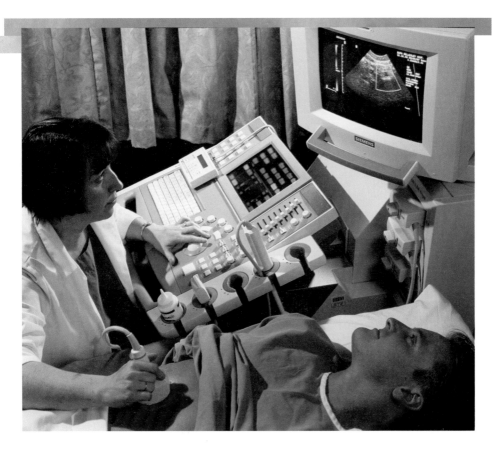

In this photograph, a health care provider uses an ultrasound to examine a man's abdomen. The ultrasound helps to examine blood flow throughout the body. Irregular blood flow can signal the presence of clots or tumors.

ULTRASOUND

Many doctors will perform an ultrasound. Ultrasound uses sound waves and their echoes to create images of a person's organs. A handheld instrument called a transducer sends out sound waves and then picks up their echoes. This information is fed to a computer and is turned into an image on a screen. An ultrasound can commonly help determine if a tumor is present in the first place, and, if it is, what the tumor's shape and texture is. It can suggest whether the tumor is benign or malignant. The test can yield a lot of information but is not invasive or painful for the patient.

CT SCAN

A computed tomography (CT) scan uses a combination of X-rays and computer technology to get amazingly detailed images of the body. It is completely painless and noninvasive, and an abdominal CT can be done in about fifteen minutes. A patient may be injected with a contrast dye to help delineate certain things, which does make the scan take a little longer.

MRI

Magnetic resonance imaging (MRI) uses a combination of radio waves and magnets to look inside the human body. As in a CT scan, a computer translates the information into a detailed image. It is a slower test than a CT scan, often taking up to an hour to perform. It may also include a contrast dye injection. It is also painless but may make a person feel claustrophobic (scared of enclosed spaces).

ANGIOGRAPHY

This is a special kind of study that looks at blood vessels. A contrast dye is injected that outlines the vessels on the image. This helps the doctor

A medical technician (above) monitors a patient undergoing an MRI of the liver. This is a painless procedure, though it involves lying very still in a tube-like structure for about an hour.

to see the specific arteries that supply blood to a certain type of liver cancer. In turn, this helps determine whether or not surgery is an option. Unlike many of the other tests, angiography can be a bit uncomfortable, as the radiologist has to insert a small catheter, or tube, into the artery leading to the liver. This is typically reached through the inner thigh. The area is numbed first, however, to help with the discomfort.

LAPAROSCOPY

In this medical procedure, a thin lighted tube is connected to a video monitor. Doctors insert the tube through a small cut in the patient's

BENIGN TUMORS

Some of the tumors found in the liver are actually benign, or harmless. Because they rarely cause any symptoms, they are typically discovered on an ultrasound examination for another suspected condition. Liver function tests show little to no abnormalities. The only way that someone might know benign tumors were there is some pain in the right upper side of the abdomen.

A hepatocellular adenoma sometimes occurs in women taking birth control pills and tends to go away with discontinuation of the medication. Focal nodular hyperplasia and hemangiomas are two other types of benign tumors found in the liver. A hemangioma is typically a mass of abnormal blood vessels. They can occur anywhere in the body, including the liver, and usually cause few symptoms. Rarely do they require treatment.

abdomen. By moving the tube around, they can get a clear image of the organs, including the liver. They can also send small instruments down the tube to remove tiny samples of tissue (biopsies) that can be examined under a microscope. Although a laparoscopy is a small operation, it is usually done on an outpatient basis (meaning no hospital stay is necessary). The patient is sedated under general anesthesia, and the area of the incision is numbed so that discomfort is minimal.

BIOPSIES

The most definitive way to tell if a patient has liver cancer is through a biopsy. A biopsy is done by taking a tiny sample of the tumor and looking at it under a microscope. Only by seeing it up close will physicians know for sure if the tumor is malignant or not.

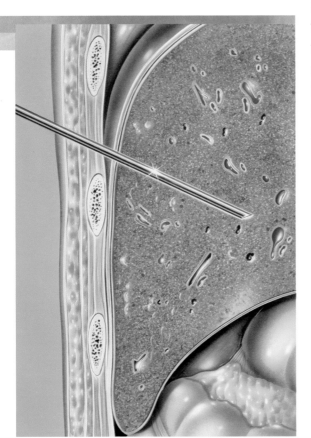

This illustration depicts a needle biopsy of liver tissue. The needle has penetrated the skin and layers of fat and muscle, passed between the ribs (the tallow spongy ovals at left), and entered the liver.

A biopsy can be obtained through an open or laparoscopic surgery, in which a sample—or even the entire mass, along with surrounding tissue—is removed. Another technique is a needle biopsy. The skin where the needle is inserted is numbed first. When the tumor is quite large or has spread throughout the liver, a physician can often insert a needle through the abdomen directly into the liver, and a small core of tissue is removed. If the tumor is smaller, then the doctor may use ultrasound or CT scanning to guide the needle to the correct spot of interest.

THE DIAGNOSIS

Once the tests are complete and the diagnosis of liver cancer has been made, there is one more step to go through before actual treatment begins: staging, or rating the severity of the cancer. Determining the stage of the cancer involves several factors, including the size of the tumor, the exact location, and if it has spread or not.

Sometimes, the cancer is staged with numbers 1 through 4 or I through IV. The higher the number, the more severe the condition and the less chance it has of responding to any form of treatment. The stages of liver cancer are:

Stage I:
A single tumor of any size that does not invade blood vessels of the liver.

Stage II:
There may be one tumor of any size or several smaller tumors (<5 centimeters) that do not invade blood vessels of the liver.

Stage III:
Several tumors, with one at least >5 cm; a tumor that has invaded the blood vessels of the liver; or a tumor that has invaded the liver's outer

covering (capsule), nearby lymph nodes, or nearby organs (other than the gallbladder).

Stage IV:
Spread of the liver cancer to other parts of the body.

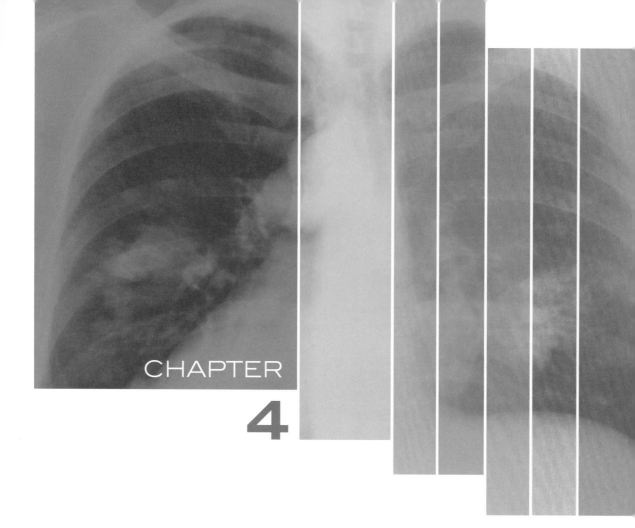

CHAPTER

4

TREATMENTS

Trying to determine the best treatment for liver cancer is a challenge for any physician. It depends on multiple factors, ranging from the patient's age, overall health, and attitude toward fighting the condition, to the stage of cancer and how much it has spread or not spread. While the best-case scenario when treating cancer is obtaining a cure, sometimes the goal has to be shifted to slowing down the growth or spread of it, or just treating the symptoms and bringing the most possible comfort to the patient.

The following are some treatments that are offered to those who have been told they have liver cancer.

SURGICAL RESECTION OR PARTIAL HEPATECTOMY

The best chance to cure liver cancer is either through transplantation or surgical resection. This surgery is quite complex and thus requires extremely skilled surgeons. With resection, surgeons try to remove every bit of the cancer. The truth is, however, is that it is rarely possible.

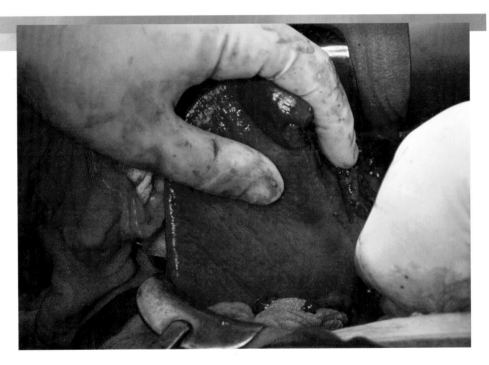

A doctor's fingers separate the right lobe of the liver, seen here, from the left. This liver is believed to have four cancerous lesions, a result of a metastatic cancer that has spread from the patient's colon.

It is more often the case that the cancer has spread to other places within or beyond the liver.

Not everyone with liver cancer is a candidate for surgery. Much of it depends on the person's overall liver health. Is the rest of the organ in good shape and working well? If so, then surgery is an option. But if there is too much cirrhosis—and four out of five liver cancer patients have cirrhosis—then the liver may not be salvageable.

TUMOR ABLATION OR EMBOLIZATION

The term "ablation" refers to the ability to destroy a tumor without actually removing it. There are several different ways to accomplish this, but it only works for patients who have several small tumors.

Hepatic artery embolization (without chemotherapy) is an option for tumors that cannot be removed surgically. It attacks the tumor by inhibiting the amount of blood that feeds it. Since most of the blood that feeds the cancer cells enters through the hepatic artery, materials are injected to block it up. A catheter is inserted into an artery in the inner thigh and sent up to the liver. A dye is used so that the physician can monitor exactly where the catheter is going. Once it is in place, small particles are injected into it, causing a blockage in the hepatic artery. Blocking this blood flow does not typically hurt healthy liver cells. They continue to get their necessary blood through the portal vein. Clearly, this technique works best for those patients who do not have hepatitis, cirrhosis, or any other liver complications.

Physicians can also perform a procedure called chemoembolization, in which chemotherapy drugs are injected directly into the blood vessels feeding a liver tumor. Another technique intended to destroy cancer cells is called radiofrequency ablation. It uses high-energy radio waves. Using an ultrasound or CT scan to guide them, doctors insert a needle-like probe into the tumor. The probe emits radio waves into the tumor, heating it up and destroying the cancer cells. In ethanol (alcohol) ablation,

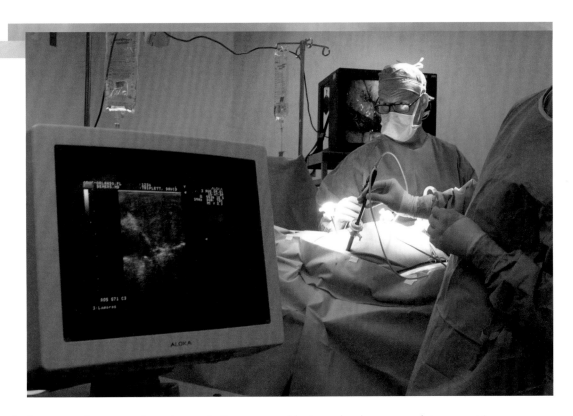

A doctor performs noninvasive radiofrequency ablation, also known as laparoscopic surgery, on a patient with liver cancer in the photo above. Watching the monitor helps the doctor guide his high-energy radio wave probe.

a needle is guided by an ultrasound or CT scan to the tumor. A needle then injects alcohol into the tumor, drying up and killing cancer cells. Another option is cryosurgery, which destroys a tumor through freezing it via an extremely cold metal probe. This works best for larger tumors. Finally, in radioembolization, the embolization process is combined with radiation therapy. Radioactive beads or oils are injected into the hepatic artery, giving off small amounts of radiation to attack the tumor sites. This is one of the newest techniques in the field of liver cancer treatment.

Cryotherapy, in which cancerous cells are frozen and killed, helps prevent the destruction of healthy cells. This is because the very cold metal probe, seen here, targets only the diseased tissue, and the procedure is quick.

None of these techniques require any kind of surgery, despite being somewhat invasive, so they are commonly used for those patients who either cannot have an operation or who are awaiting a transplant.

RADIATION THERAPY

In radiation therapy, the killing agent is a series of high-energy rays. Once again, there are several different ways that they can be used to attack and kill those cancer cells.

External beam radiation therapy sends radiation to the cancer from outside the body. It can be used to shrink the tumor and relieve pain. The biggest complication with this method is that if the doses are high enough to kill the cancer, then they also injure healthy liver tissue. If the dose is low enough not to endanger the healthy tissue, then it usually isn't strong enough to kill the cancer.

In three-dimensional conformal radiation therapy (3DCRT), the same radiation therapy is used, except it is coupled with complex computers so that the exact location of the tumor can be determined. This time, the patient is put into a body mold to help him or her keep still while the radiation beams are sent out to the tumor from several directions. This technique attempts to protect the healthy liver tissue.

CHEMOTHERAPY

Chemotherapy uses drugs to kill cancer. Some are injected, and others are taken by mouth. Once in the bloodstream, they go to all parts of the body, which can help with a cancer that has spread. Sadly, chemotherapy is not particularly effective for liver cancer. It tends to resist most of the

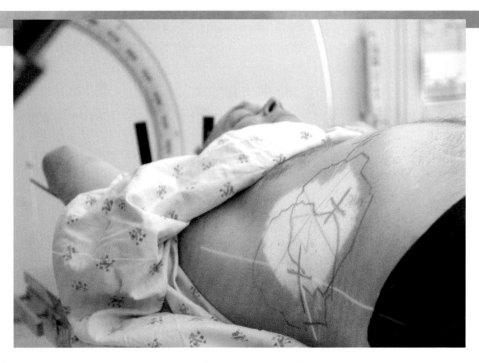

This liver cancer patient awaits radiation therapy. The area around his liver has been outlined with paint, showing the radiologist where the beam of radiation should be directed.

medications used, and chemotherapy does not appear to extend a person's life by any significant time at all.

To further complicate matters, chemotherapy kills not only cancer cells but also normal cells, which tends to result in some very unpleasant side effects. How severe and frequent these side effects are depends on the type of drug, how much is taken, and how long it is taken. Side effects typically include nausea, vomiting, loss of appetite, loss of hair, and

LIVER TRANSPLANTS

Today, more than seventeen thousand people are on a national waiting list to receive a new liver. The more serious the condition, the higher the patient's name is on the list. There are far more people needing a liver than there are those donating livers. Thousands of liver transplants are performed each year in the United States. While many of the people getting a transplant are doing it because of cirrhosis, a person with liver cancer that has not yet metastasized is also a candidate, though the waiting list for a new liver can be very long.

A living donor can actually share his or her liver with another person. A section of a healthy person's liver is transplanted into the patient. The partial livers of both the donor and the recipient will then grow back to the necessary size because the liver is able to regenerate. Although such surgery may last up to twelve hours and require a three-week hospital stay, it is an effective option for many. Five years after the surgery, 75 percent of patients do well, especially if they received the transplant from a living donor.

mouth sores. The chemo can also impair the bone marrow's production of blood cells. This means that a person undergoing chemotherapy has a much higher chance of developing an infection due to a shortage of white blood cells. It also means a bigger risk of bleeding or bruising after a cut or injury due to a shortage of platelets. Fatigue and shortness of breath may also result because of low red blood cell counts. Patients usually require red blood cell and platelet transfusions during chemotherapy.

A FEW ALTERNATIVES

Along with the traditional medical treatments such as the ones already described, some people may also choose to use alternative therapies to cope with their liver cancer. Patients can use complementary medicine as adjunctive (additional or secondary) therapy, not as primary treatment for cancer. Alternative treatments and therapies aren't used as cures. Instead, they are designed to help the patient feel better, reduce stress, and relieve certain symptoms. Some of the possible alternative therapies are:

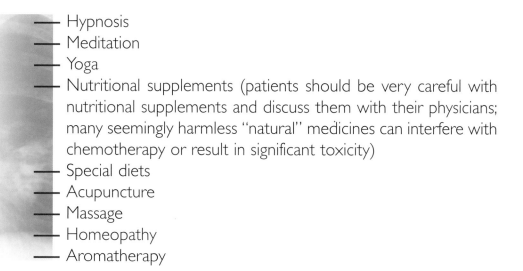

— Hypnosis
— Meditation
— Yoga
— Nutritional supplements (patients should be very careful with nutritional supplements and discuss them with their physicians; many seemingly harmless "natural" medicines can interfere with chemotherapy or result in significant toxicity)
— Special diets
— Acupuncture
— Massage
— Homeopathy
— Aromatherapy

Stress reduction techniques like exercise and yoga are an important part of both battling and recovering from cancer. Physical activity helps strengthen and restore the body, mind, and spirit.

Patients interested in alternative therapies should first check with their physician. While most complementary therapies are safe, it is important to make sure that the doctor has no objections to any of them. Typically, any alternative care that promises a cure, urges the patient to discontinue other conventional medical treatment, or involves going to another country for treatment should be viewed with skepticism and considered very carefully.

Some cancer centers offer a variety of other options, including couple and family counseling, stress management, relaxation techniques, deep-breathing lessons, guided imagery sessions, spiritual support, humor therapy, and support groups. Physical therapy is important for patients with liver cancer going through anticancer therapy. It includes a regular exercise program, along with stretching exercises to increase flexibility and massage. Pain management is commonly part of treatment because liver cancer can cause a great deal of physical discomfort, as can some of the treatment processes. Pain is usually controlled through different kinds of medication.

WHAT ABOUT CLINICAL TRIALS?

"Clinical trials" is just a technical term for experimental study of promising new medical treatments. Clinical trials are performed when there is good reason to believe that a new medication, tool, or treatment process may help patients. Researchers look to see if these new possibilities will be better than current options, what side effects each one might have, and how to balance the new treatment's effectiveness with its potential side effects. The studies are performed with small groups of interested patients. Clinical trials have helped many doctors discover new ways to diagnose and treat many different diseases. They focus on new drugs not yet approved by the federal government, nondrug treatments, medical procedures, herbs and vitamins, and new tools and procedures developed to relieve symptoms or improve overall comfort in patients. Before trying new medications in human patients, new therapies have been extensively tested on animals and in preclinical models.

Clinical trials follow a series of four steps, referred to as phases. Each one addresses a different set of questions.

Phase I: This part of the study addresses the safety of a new drug in a small number of patients. It focuses on the best way to use it and how much of it is safe to administer. It begins with low doses, which are then increased until negative side effects appear (the "dose-limiting toxicity") or the desired positive effect appears. Once the proper dosage is established, the drug can move to Phase II trials. In general, only patients with very advanced or refractory disease are eligible for Phase I trials.

Phase II: This part of the study tests to see if the drug actually works. It is usually done with a larger group of patients than that used in the first phase of testing. If the treatment proves to be effective at the dosage established in the first phase, then the researchers can then try this medication in a larger group of patients in a Phase III trial.

Phase III: This part of the study offers the experimental treatment to a much larger group of patients, often thousands at a time. Generally, patients are randomly assigned to receive the standard-of-care (best available) treatment or the standard-of-care plus the new experimental medication. The patients are divided up into smaller groups, called control and experimental groups. The control patients get the standard treatment, while the others get the new one being studied in the trial. They are all closely watched in order to see what changes and side effects occur. At this point, the researchers may have enough evidence to get the U.S. Food and Drug Administration (FDA), the federal agency responsible for regulating prescription medications, among other things, to approve the new treatment for the general public.

Once the FDA has approved the drug and makes it generally available to people, it continues to be studied. This way, experts can learn as much as possible about the drug's unforeseen short- and longer-term effects and overall safety.

Taking part in a clinical trial is a big decision. It has been widely proven, though, that patients enrolled in clinical trials actually do much better than those who are not treated in national studies. If you choose to participate, you or your doctor can choose to remove you from the study at any time. You will be closely monitored and receive a great deal of one-on-one attention. However, it also carries some risk, since there is no way of knowing if the treatment being studied will be effective or not. Anyone interested in being part of a clinical trial should first talk it over with his or her physician and other cancer-care team members. Questions to ask before agreeing to join the study include:

- What is the purpose of the study?
- What kinds of tests and treatments will I have to undergo in the study?
- How could this study affect my day-to-day life?
- Will I hurt my chances for recovery or a cure by taking part in this study?
- What if my health declines during the study?
- What are the potential side effects, and how can I manage them?
- Is there any cost to me for this study? Is it free?

— Do I have to stay in the hospital during the trial?

— If I'm harmed by this research, then what kind of treatment will I receive?

— How do you protect my confidentiality?

How do you find out about clinical trials that focus on liver cancer? Contact the American Cancer Society (www.cancer.org), which has a free matching service between trials and patients.

WHAT HAPPENS AFTER TREATMENT?

Once treatment has ended, patients continue to be seen in follow-up appointments for some time. These visits generally include a review of symptoms, physical exams, and additional blood tests or imaging studies. The follow-ups are done to make sure that the patient is healing, as well as to check for any signs of recurrence or negative side effects from the treatment processes. Some side effects fade away immediately, while others can linger for a few weeks or months. Some can even turn out to be permanent.

In addition to visits with a physician, many post-treatment patients decide to make some basic lifestyle changes. For example, they may stop drinking alcohol or smoking. They might start eating healthier and getting additional exercise. Now that they have a second chance at life, they want to make the most of it.

TEN GREAT QUESTIONS
TO ASK YOUR DOCTOR

Cancer can be an intimidating diagnosis, so learning as much as possible about the condition is one way patients can feel like they have more control over the situation. Here are some questions to ask a physician if you or someone you love is diagnosed with cancer:

1. May I have a copy of the pathology report to look over?

2. Has my cancer spread beyond the liver, and how would we know if it has?

3. What stage is the cancer at this point?

4. Can this tumor be eliminated through surgery?

5. What are the treatment options? Are there clinical trials available? Should we consider taking part in one?

6. Which techniques do you recommend and why?

7. What are the risks of each kind of treatment?

8. What are the chances of the cancer returning after treatment?

9. How will this condition and the treatment affect me or my loved one on a daily basis?

10. What are the chances of entering remission and enjoying a complete recovery?

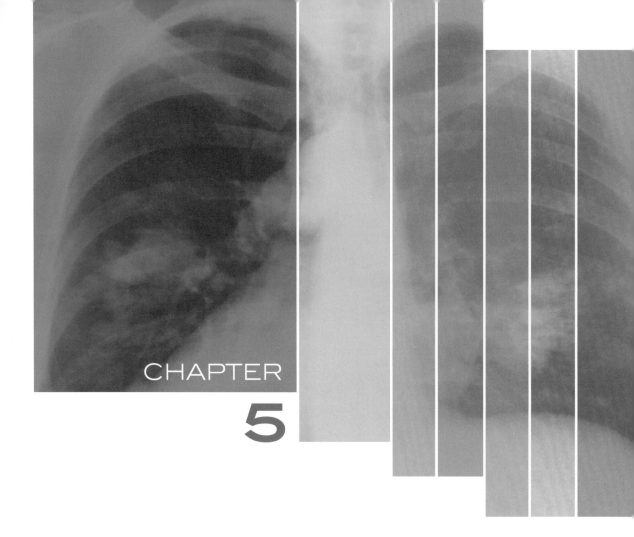

CUTTING-EDGE RESEARCH

Since liver cancer is quite serious and has few effective treatments, there is a great deal of research being performed to develop more promising options. Researchers are constantly looking for better ways to detect liver cancer, treat it, and even defeat it entirely.

RADIOEMBOLIZATION

The technique of radioembolization is still a very new approach. Specialists at Jefferson Medical College's Kimmel Cancer Center in Philadelphia, Pennsylvania, have recently done an eighteen-month study

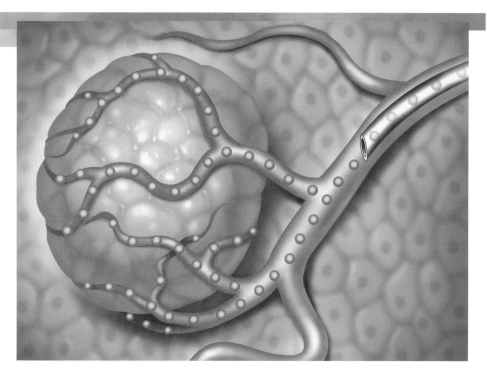

In selective internal radiation therapy, SIR-Spheres are used to attack liver tumors that can't be surgically removed. Millions of tiny polymer beads or microspheres deliver targeted, internal radiation through the bloodstream directly to tumors (like the yellow mass seen here).

on what happens when tiny beads with small amounts of radiation are injected into a liver cancer patient's hepatic artery. The process was just recently approved by the FDA for use in patients who have liver cancer that cannot be removed through surgery.

Radioembolization uses thirty times more of these radioactive beads than other procedures, sending millions of them through a catheter directly to the site of the cancer. While it doesn't cure the condition, it does help to shrink the tumors and often allows the patient to live longer. "This extends the numbers of patients who can be treated with

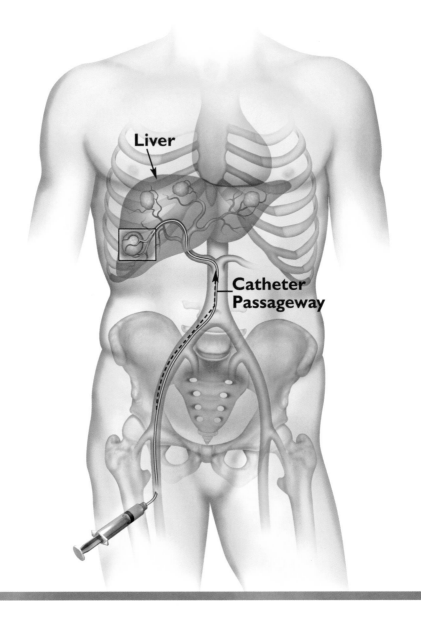

Liver

Catheter Passageway

SIR-Spheres are delivered to liver tumors after being injected into a catheter through the groin, as seen here. The catheter carries the microspheres to the liver, where they enter the bloodstream and are carried to the tumor.

Sirtex is the company that makes SIR-Spheres (www. sirtex.com). It believes that microspheres will become the standard treatment for liver cancer in the near future.

this much safer treatment," said Dr. Brian Carr, professor of medical oncology at Jefferson Medical College. "It's much safer because these patients don't get chemotherapy side effects such as nausea and hair loss, and they generally don't need to be in the hospital except for the day of treatment, which is usually every three months. The immediate objective is to get patients to live longer and ultimately a cure." In an online article in *Science Daily*, Carr added, "[M]any of these patients would have their liver tumors shrunken to the point where surgery is possible. Some may be able to have a cure." A technique similar to radioembolization involves the injection of a special kind of radioactive oil into the hepatic artery.

CONTROLLING BLOOD LOSS

Some new avenues of liver cancer treatment currently being explored include using different tools during cancer surgery. Since the liver is so rich with blood, surgery may involve significant blood loss. The typical liver surgery patient could need between 5 and 10 units of blood during the operation. However, two new tools appear to decrease blood loss significantly. The first one is a tool called a CUSA (cavitron ultrasonic surgical aspirator). It uses ultrasound to aspirate, or suck out, the liver cells, rather then cutting them out with a scalpel. The second tool is a technique developed by TissueLink Medical, Inc., that uses a fluid to deliver radio-frequency energy directly to tissue. The fluid controls the temperature where the energy meets the tissue, allowing tissue to seal without burning or tearing, resulting in less blood loss. Blood vessels are sealed before they can begin to bleed.

NEW IDEAS AND BETTER ANSWERS

Other ideas being explored include developing a hepatitis C vaccine, blood tests that are able to detect liver cancer much earlier, new methods to treat or shrink tumors before surgery, and treatments geared to replace the DNA of damaged cells. A study published in the *Cancer Research Journal* states that researchers were working on a compound that protects against the development of liver cancer in the first place. It has been used only in lab animals to date, but it shows promise. It is hoped that the compound will be able to stimulate certain enzymes in the body to remove toxic substances from liver cells. In a National Institutes of Health (NIH) article, the leader of the project, National Institute of Environmental Health Sciences director David A. Schwartz, stated, "The results show that the potency of this compound is more than 100 times as great as that of other chemopreventive agents in protecting against cancer . . . This protective effect, combined with the compound's anti-inflammatory properties, make it an exciting avenue for the prevention of other diseases as well."

There is a growing interest in how many liver cancer surgeries could be performed laparoscopically (except in the cases of large tumors when open surgeries are preferred to increase the chances of the complete removal of the cancerous growth). This involves the making

The president of Singapore, S. R. Nathan, operates a laparoscopic surgery simulator on an artificial abdomen during an official state visit to the Clinical Training and Research Centre in Perth, Australia.

of a small incision in the abdomen, then inserting instruments into it to remove the part of the liver that is diseased. By operating this way, there is far less blood loss, less pain after surgery, and a quicker recovery.

Radiation therapy is often difficult with liver cancer because it damages healthy liver tissue at the same time that it attacks cancerous tissue. One possible solution being explored is using drugs called radiosensitizers, which help make the cancer more vulnerable to the radiation, necessitating lower doses of radiation and the sparing of healthy cells.

Finding better answers to the grave threat of liver cancer is a high priority for many researchers, surgeons, and medical doctors. It is an even higher priority for the thousands of people on the liver transplant list and the thousands more who are diagnosed each year with this devastating disease. While new answers are being sought, the best advice any medical authority can give to people is to do everything possible to prevent ever needing this kind of technology in the first place. Prevention through lifestyle changes such as healthy eating, exercise, alcohol avoidance, and stress reduction may, in the end, represent our best hope for beating liver cancer.

GLOSSARY

aflatoxin A type of mold that grows on peanuts, nuts, corn, and grain.

alpha-fetoprotein A protein derived from the liver that, when elevated, can be suggestive of liver cancer.

ascites Abnormal amounts of fluid building up in the abdomen.

benign Noncancerous.

bile A fluid made in the liver that is important to digesting fats.

circulatory system The body's system of distributing blood throughout the body.

cirrhosis A liver disease that involves scarring and damage of the liver cells and interruption of blood flow throughout the liver.

hepatic artery The artery that brings blood rich in oxygen to the liver.

hepatic portal vein The vein that carries nutrients to the liver from the intestines.

hepatitis Disease of the liver causing inflammation.

hepatocytes Liver cells.

jaundice Yellowing of the skin and eyes caused by the buildup of bilirubin (a waste product excreted in bile) in the blood.

lobe A section of the liver.

lobules Smaller divisions within a lobe.

lymphatic system Vessels and nodes that comprise the body's immune system to recognize and attack foreign substances.

malignant Cancerous.

metastasize Spread to other parts of the body.

FOR MORE INFORMATION

American Cancer Society (ACS)
P.O. Box 22718
Oklahoma City, OK 73123-1718
(800) ACS-2345 (227-2345)
Web site: http://www.cancer.org
The ACS is the nationwide voluntary health organization dedicated to eliminating cancer as a major health problem through research, education, advocacy, and service.

American Liver Foundation (ALF)
75 Maiden Lane, Suite 603
New York, NY 10038
(800) GO-LIVER (465-4837)
Web site: http://www.liverfoundation.org
The ALF is the nation's leading nonprofit organization promoting liver health and disease prevention. It provides research, education, and advocacy for those affected by liver-related diseases, including hepatitis, cirrhosis, and liver cancer.

National Cancer Institute
6116 Executive Boulevard, Room 3036A
Bethesda, MD 20892-8322
(800) 4-CANCER (422-6237)
Web site: http://www.cancer.gov
The National Cancer Institute is the federal government's principal
   agency for cancer research and training.

National Foundation for Transplants (NFT)
5350 Poplar Avenue, Suite 430
Memphis, TN 38119
(800) 489-3863
Web site: http://www.transplants.org
The NFT provides advocacy, support, and financial assistance to
   transplant candidates and recipients.

United Network for Organ Sharing (UNOS)
P.O. Box 2484
Richmond, VA 23218
(888) 894-6361
Web site: http://www.unos.org
The UNOS facilitates organ sharing among transplant centers, organ
   procurement organizations, and histocompatibility laboratories
   across the United States.

WEB SITES

Due to the changing nature of Internet links, Rosen Publishing has
developed an online list of Web sites related to the subject of this book.
This site is updated regularly. Please use this link to access the list:

http://www.rosenlinks.com/cms/live

FOR FURTHER READING

Caldwell, Wilma A. *Cancer Information for Teens: Health Tips About Cancer Awareness, Prevention, Diagnosis, and Treatment.* Detroit, MI: Omnigraphics, 2004.

Feuerstein, Michael, and Patricia Findley. *The Cancer Survivor's Guide: The Essential Handbook to Life After Cancer.* New York, NY: Marlowe & Co., 2006.

Hobbs, Valerie. *Defiance.* New York, NY: Farrar, Straus, and Giroux, 2004.

Keane, Maureen, and Daniella Chace. *What to Eat If You Have Cancer.* New York, NY: McGraw-Hill, 2006.

Mareck, Amy. *Fighting for My Life: Growing Up with Cancer.* Minneapolis, MN: Fairview Press, 2007.

Silverstein, Alvin, et al. *Cancer: Conquering a Deadly Disease.* Minneapolis, MN: Twenty-First Century Books, 2004.

Stewart, Gail. *Alexandra Scott: Champion for Cancer Research.* Farmington Hills, MI: KidHaven Press, 2006.

Wyborny, Sheila. *Science on the Edge: Cancer Treatments.* Farmington Hills, MI: Blackbirch Press, 2005.

BIBLIOGRAPHY

Abou-Alfa, Ghassan K., and Ronald DeMatteo. *100 Questions and Answers About Liver Cancer.* Sudbury, MA: Jones & Bartlett Publishers, Inc., 2005.

American Cancer Society. "Liver Cancer Detailed Guide." Retrieved March 2008 (http://www.cancer.org/docroot/CRI/CRI_2_3x.asp?dt=25).

American Cancer Society. "What Is Liver Cancer?" Retrieved March 2008 (http://www.cancer.org/docroot/CRI/content/CRI_2_2_1X_What_is_liver_cancer_25.asp).

American Cancer Society. "What's New in Liver Cancer Research?" Retrieved March 2008 (http://www.cancer.org/docroot/cri/content/cri_2_2_7x_whats_new_in_liver_cancer_research_25.asp).

Campbell, Kalli, MS, RD. "Nutrition Therapy for Liver Cancer." Liver Cancer Center. Retrieved March 2008 (http://www.cancercenter.com/liver-cancer/nutritional-therapy.cfm).

Chopra, Sanjiv. *The Liver Book: A Comprehensive Guide to Diagnosis, Treatment, and Recovery.* New York, NY: Atria, 2001.

CNN.com. "Liver Cancer." Retrieved March 2008 (http://www.cnn.com/HEALTH/library/DS/00399.html).

Curley, Steven A., ed. *Liver Cancer.* New York, NY: Springer, 1998.

Fong, Tse-Ling M. C. "Hepatocellular Carcinoma." MedicineNet.com. Retrieved April 2008 (http://www.medicinenet.com/liver_cancer/article.htm).

KGET. "Removing Portions of Diseased Liver." Retrieved March 2008 (http://www.kget.com/news/local/story.aspx?content_id=a785dbd8-cad3-4330-b217-4549d7024d9a).

MayoClinic.com. "Liver Cancer." Retrieved March 2008 (http://www.mayoclinic.com/health/liver-cancer/DS00399).

MayoClinic.com. "Radiofrequency Ablation for Cancer." Retrieved March 2008 (http://www.mayoclinic.org/radiofrequency-ablation/liver.html).

National Cancer Institute. "What You Need to Know About Liver Cancer." Retrieved March 2008 (http://www.cancer.gov/cancertopics/wyntk/liver).

Parker, James N., and Philip M. Parker, eds. *The Official Patient's Sourcebook on Adult Primary Liver Cancer.* San Diego, CA: Icon Health Publications, 2002.

Peterson, John. "New Compound May Protect Against Liver Cancer." NIH News, February 2006. Retrieved March 2008 (http://www.nih.gov/news/pr/feb2006/niehs-15.htm).

Science Daily. "New Trial to Test Radiation-Emitting Beads Against Advanced Liver Cancer." February 2008. Retrieved March 2008 (http://www.sciencedaily.com/releases/2008/02/080212155734.htm).

UCSF Medical Center. "Liver Cancer: Signs and Symptoms." Retrieved March 2008 (http://www.ucsfhealth.org/adult/medical_services/cancer/liver/conditions/livercancer/signs.html).

Vann, Madeline. "Genetic Variation Doubles Risk of Liver Cancer." Health on the Net Foundation. Retrieved March 2008 (http://www.hon.ch/News/HSN/611312.html).

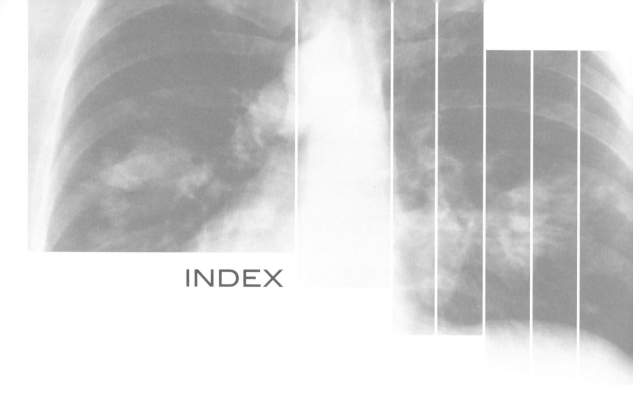

INDEX

ABOUT THE AUTHOR

Tamra B. Orr is the author of numerous nonfiction books. She has written on a number of medical and health topics but knows cancer up close and personal as she has lost four of the most important people in her life to the disease. Orr has a degree in secondary education and public health from Ball State University. She lives in the beautiful Pacific Northwest with her husband and four kids.

PHOTO CREDITS

Cover, p. 1 © Kenneth Eward/Photo Researchers, Inc.; cover corner photo, pp. 4–5 © Punchstock; back cover and throughout © National Cancer Institute; p. 5 Chris Anderson/Aurora/Getty Images; p. 8 Illustration © 2008 Nucleus Medical Art. All rights reserved. www.nucleusinc.com; p. 10 © John M. Daugherty/Photo Researchers, Inc.; p. 13 © Susumu Nishinaga/Photo Researchers, Inc.; pp. 18, 31 © John Bavosi/Photo Researchers, Inc.; p. 19 © Steve Gschmeissner/Photo Researchers, Inc.; p. 21 © Arthur Glauberman/Photo Researchers, Inc.; p. 26 © www.istockphoto.com/Joseph Abbott; p. 27 © Geoff Tompkinson/Photo Researchers, Inc.; p. 29 © Phanie/Photo Researchers, Inc.; p. 35 © B. Slaven/Custom Medical Stock Photo; p. 37 krtphotos/Newscom; p. 38 © Art & Science, Inc./Custom Medical Stock Photo; pp. 39, 42 © AP Images; pp. 49, 50 Courtesy of Sirtex Medical, Inc.; p. 53 Tony Ashby/AFP/Getty Images.

Designer: Evelyn Horovicz; Photo Researcher: Amy Feinberg